THE EUROPEAN UNION AND SPACE

FOSTERING APPLICATIONS, MARKETS AND INDUSTRIAL COMPETITIVENESS

Communication to the Council
and the European Parliament

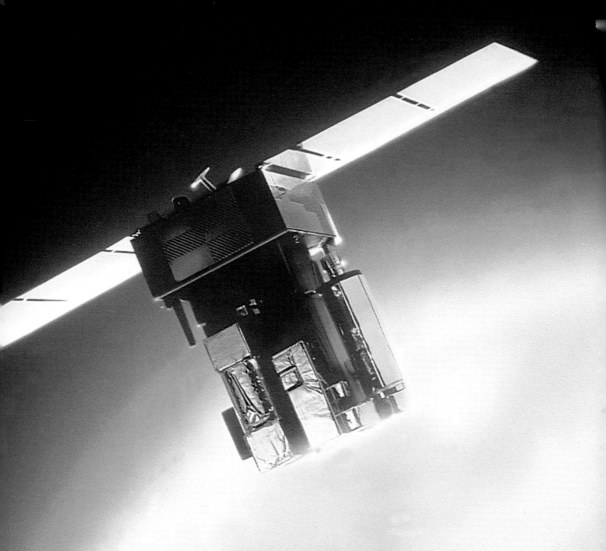

Edith CRESSON, Member of the Commission responsible for Research, Innovation, Education, Training and Youth
DG XII - Science, Research and Development

Martin BANGEMANN, Member of the Commission responsible for Industrial Affairs, Information and Telecommunications Technologies
DG III - Industry

Neil KINNOCK, Member of the Commission responsible for Transport including Trans-European Networks
DG VII - Transport

Contact: M. Herbert Allgeier Tel. +32 2 295 40 55 - Fax. +32 2 296 29 80

A EUROPEAN SPACE STRATEGY FOR THE EUROPEAN UNION

At the drawn of the 21st century, after forty years of operating in space, its exploitation has developed at an impressive rate, progressively generating a whole series of applications whose results have surpassed all expectations, whether they be in the domain of telecommunications, navigation, transport or observation of the Earth from space. Satellites have changed our life on earth. Some of them are veritable guardians of the peace and protect our security. Others are gradually weaving around our planet the fabric of the future information society. Others again are building up our understanding of the Earth's environment.

Space takes its place at the approach of the year 2000 as one of the key economic, technological, scientific and cultural activities of the coming century.

Against that background the European Commission intends to play its part in this new adventure within the framework of a European space strategy based on close cooperation with all the actors in space - the European Union, the Member States and their national agencies, the European Space Agency, Eumetsat, industry, the operators and the users.

Edith CRESSON
Member of the Commission

Martin BANGEMANN
Member of the Commission

Neil KINNOCK
Member of the Commission

SUMMARY

This Communication aims to explain to Council and Parliament how the Commission sees the role of the European Union in space taking into account the recent evolution of the sector, to seek agreement on this approach and to outline the main priorities for its future action. These priorities will lead subsequently to specific proposals to be submitted to the relevant bodies.

The main lines proposed for action could be summarised as follows:

○ In the field of Space Telecommunications: develop a favourable legislative and normative environment to the benefit of European industry for the development of this important market and sustain the development of new technologies through a vigorous R&D effort.

○ In the field of Space Navigation; ensure that Europe has a position commensurate with its strategic and commercial ambitions in this rapidly growing application. The essential elements of the proposed action are: development of new applications; their demonstration in areas of significant interest such as air navigation; bringing together potential users; promoting relevant R&D efforts.

○ In the field of Earth Observation: whereas the transition has still to be made from a science-driven technique to a market driven technology, actions should be concentrated on demonstrating new applications with a relevant R&D effort to sustain it, involving users, creating the appropriate regulatory environment for its further development.

Beyond these three major applications the Commission should use its competence in terms of external trade; internal market and international cooperation to cover horizontal aspects such as ensuring a vigorous presence of Europe in space launch services, in the standardisation of space components and in establishing cooperative activities with foreign nations.

Finally, the Commission should encourage a coordinated approach to dual use technologies, should examine how to improve funding mechanisms for the space industry and should, from an institutional point of view, reinforce its ties with the European Space Agency.

TABLE OF CONTENTS

INTRODUCTION

Space is no longer only a tool to explore the universe and to bring man to new frontiers. Even if these aspects remain important, space has now also strategic and economic dimensions. Space applications have opened new markets which are significant on the world trade scene and which have also brought new ways to satisfy human needs.

As space contributes both to the industrial competitiveness of Europe and to the improvement in the quality of life of its citizens, the European Union cannot be indifferent about space developments. This does not mean that the European Union should substitute for relevant bodies, notably the European Space Agency, in formulating the European space policy but the European Union should contribute to the full development of the space policy and take into account the space dimension in the formulation and implementation of the policies mentioned in the Treaty.

The European Union has had an interest for the space field for about a decade. The Commission's 1988 communication on space[1] established the principle of a Union involvement in Europe's space activity and outlined its role which had to be complementary to that of the European Space Agency (ESA).

At Union level, the development and demonstration of space applications have received increasing attention in the 4th Framework Programme for Research and Technology Development and Demonstration (1994-1998)[3] as well as in the implementation of a number of the Union's policies.

The Commission, as part of its continued dialogue with the industry, has convened a High-level Group of industrialists to help and define actions intended to promote a dynamic and competitive space industry in Europe.

Since the presentation of the last Communication "The European Union and Space: challenges, opportunities and new actions" of 23 September 1992[2], the overall international scenario has greatly evolved and new important events have occurred, requiring an update of the Commission's position in the space field:

The emerging information society, together with technological developments, have opened up new perspectives for the use of space, which is of great socio-economic importance because of the inherent trans-border character of satellite services.

The markets for space applications are developing fast, particularly in the areas of telecommunications and navigation; while Earth Observation is emerging from the realm of science towards an increased role of the market. Simultaneously, world competition on the markets for satellites and launch services is becoming increasingly intense and global.

The restructuring process within European industry has made some progress, but at the same time their USA competitors have evolved towards greatly increased concentration.

The ESA Ministerial Council of Toulouse in 1995 has taken important decisions, in the field of launchers and space infrastructure, which will affect the funding of application programmes. It also launched an assessment of ESA's industrial policy which may lead to its revision and which may relate to some of the Union fields of competence.

This Communication takes into account the conclusions of the Council meeting of Research Ministers on 29.4.93[4], the European Parliament Resolution of 6.5.94[5] and the ESA ministerial Resolutions on 10.11.92 and 20.10.95, as well as the discussions during the European Space Forum on 6.11.95, the views expressed by the Space Advisory Group (SAG) and the report of the Industry High Level Group of 30.1.96. The next three sections set the general context of space and it applications within Europe. Sections 5 to 7 deal with the three most important space applications, while sections 8 to 13 cover some horizontal policy issues.

1 COM(88) 417 final
2 COM(92) 360 final
3 O.J. L 126, 18.5.1994
4 PV/CONS 22 - RECH 22 - 6280/93 of 6.5.1993
5 O.J. C 205/467, 25.7.1994

THE IMPORTANCE OF SPACE TO EUROPE

For more than thirty years, space has proved to be of crucial strategic, socio-economic and scientific importance. The major economic powers have implemented programmes to enable the parties involved, essentially the public authorities and industry, to demonstrate and exploit the potential of space technologies.

The creation of ESRO, ELDO and then ESA, alongside national agencies and institutions, have allowed the development of a wide range of technological capabilities and an important industrial infrastructure. These efforts have put Europe at the forefront of the space field, though the levels of European spending cannot be compared to those of the US or the former USSR.

As a result of this investment effort, there are now in Europe some 350 industrial companies with a degree of involvement in space activities, from the prime contractors to the first, second or third-level subcontractors and suppliers. Taking a wide definition, this sector generates up to 8 bn ECU and represents over 30,000 industrial jobs, with a further 9,000 in related institutions (space agencies, research centres, Universities, etc.). As comparison there are about 200,000 jobs in the space business in the US.

World space budgets (MECU)

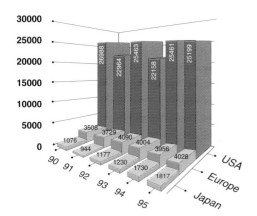

To fully appreciate the economic impor-tance of this industry, one must see it as a key element in a much larger value added chain. Typically, the bulk of that chain is made up of services, which together with the ground and user segments may represent more than ten times the value of the spacecraft and launchers. A European strategy towards the development of space activities, as proposed below, must therefore avoid a narrow concept of the space industry which would be limited to the space segment manufacturers, and include these related sectors.

Other than the economic stakes, Europe has a strategic interest in the development of, and access to, space applications which have an impact on policy fields such as the information society, environment, agricult-ure, trans-European networks, regional policy, development aid etc. In this context the Union can place space techniques in the proper policy framework and may play a key role of pioneer customer in those applications which are potentially interesting to the implementation of its policies and to the fulfilment of user's needs.

Europe's space activities, like in other sectors, are more concentrated in some of the member states. The downstream industries and services concern a much wider variety of countries and regions, and the same is true for the main space applications. Indeed, it can be said that space systems ignore political boundaries, they equally favour all European regions, in particular less favoured regions, and, thereby, social and economic cohesion within the Union, taking into account the importance of space technologies for improving infrastructures (telecommuni-cations, land use, urban development, ...) or quality of life (broadcasting, water management, ...).

This communication addresses the main issues for which there is an immediate Union interest and potential for action.

Space science and manned space activities, although important from the strategic and industrial points of view, are essentially within the remit of the European Space Agency (ESA), national agencies and the Member States. In any case, complementarity and synergy between those efforts and Union policies such as research and technological development (RTD), human resources or external cooperation will be actively sought and exploited in order to sustain and potentiate all the sectors where Europe is already or may become competitive.

In particular the use of the International Space Station, as a big scientific facility, should be considered in the imple-mentation of the future Framework Programmes.

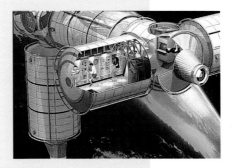

THE SPACE INDUSTRY:
OVERALL ISSUES.

A changing environment:
transition to a global information society

The space industry, including the ground segment and related services industries, is having to cope with a number of external changes which impact on its operating environment:

○ The end of the geo-political context which had fuelled the growth of the sector for decades, as well as the economic slowdown and budgetary policies of recent years. This meant that, for the first time in its history, space employment has fallen in the last three years.

○ The increased globalisation and opening of the international marketplace and the emergence of new competitors. This situation is exacerbated by a current excess industrial capacity resulting from the above mentioned factors.

○ Also at global scale, technological developments and the movement towards the global information society have opened new application areas (satellite personal communications, multimedia, navigation etc.) whose importance was unforeseen only a few years ago.

Some of these factors may be of a temporary nature, others will require permanent changes in the way the industry operates and in the role of public powers in this field. Industry is conscious of the fact that its present structures will have to be adapted in response to those changes, but it needs clear signals from the public authorities, as to what the new environment will be.

Turnover of the European space industry by origin
million ECU

	1991	1992	1993	1994	1995*	1996*	1997*
National civilian R&D	773	899	664	685	705	678	698
ESA	1,396	1,749	1,462	1,470	1,653	1,427	1,363
Commercial	972	1,021	1,048	1,261	1,333	1,589	1,541
Defence	248	285	265	350	414	419	480
TOTAL	3,389	3,954	3,439	3,766	4,105	4,113	4,082

* forecasts   Source: CNES - Eurospace

The growing space applications and downstream markets.

The level of activity in the European space industry has experienced an interruption of its growth after 1992, which can be put down mainly to the evolution of government funding. Meanwhile, their commercial and defence sales have experienced a moderate increase.

These figures show (in spite of significant differences between countries) that for the space industry commercial applications are only one element, not for the time being the dominant one. However, there is a clear trend for the market element to gain in importance: from 29% of the industry's turnover in 1991, to a forecast 38% in 1997.

As already pointed out, in the market-oriented space applications the space segment is often only the tip of the iceberg. The bulk of business and employment are to be found in the downstream, applications-related industries and services which are, furthermore, growing at a faster rate than that of the space segment. This should not hide, however, the importance of the space segment as a

Worldwide civilian space market: prospects for 1996-2005
billion ECU

	Satellite communications		Satellite positioning	Remote sensing
	Traditional geostationary	PCS and broadband*		
Space segment inc. launch and operation	47-64	12	0.8-1	10-13
Ground segment and user terminals	47-70	100	27-38	4-5
Services and applications	> 100	>200	30-45	8-13

* *Satellite personal communications services (PCS) and broadband (multimedia) services are expected to come on stream in the next ten years.*

Source: ESA - Euroconsult

strategic element in the whole chain. The fact that Europe has a prominent position in the space segment gives the industry an important leverage in the application markets, enabling it to sell complete systems and services to international customers. Moreover, space segment manufacturers often play a key role in the design of the entire application systems and in the definition of the technical options and standards to be used by the corresponding ground segment.

The table above gives the estimates of the market prospects for the main space applications.

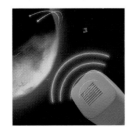

A sector of worldwide competition

The position of the European industry in the space markets which are open to competition varies between a market share of more than 50% in space launch services, thanks to the Ariane programme, and 5% or less in some categories of ground equipment.

In the satellite manufacturing sector, which has a strategic position in the chain, Europe is currently achieving 20-25% of prime contractorships at world level, the remaining going to the US industry. More significantly, virtually all the proposals for the new global and regional communications systems (personal and broadband services) are US led, with Europe only now starting a late reaction. The European industry's role as a subcontractor, and equipments supplier has increased, however, as has Japan's. Japan already leads Europe in the ground segment markets and, in the medium term, plans to become a satellite prime contractor and to enter the commercial launch market.

Competition in the latter market field has become stronger, with the emergence of new suppliers such as Russia, China and Ukraine. The market for the launch of small spacecraft is also gaining in importance, which may prompt the entering of emerging space powers such as India or Israel.

Finally, in the remote sensing market, the offers are mutiplying from a number of suppliers beyond the traditional ones, and the first commercially-driven missions are being planned in the US.

The conditions for industrial competitiveness

European initiative needs to be strengthened in the emerging fields such as satellite navigation, PCS, multimedia and broadband communications, building on confirmed European strengths such as the experience gained in Ka band technology or in direct satellite broadcasting. As already emphasised by the Commission[6], it is important to capitalise on the European space industry's capacity to translate its R&D investment into innovative products. One can say, in fact, that innovation is built into this sector, but this is not enough to allay concerns that European competitiveness relative to the (mostly American) market leaders may deteriorate further.

Apart from the fact that the US has long benefited from a genuine single market, their advantage is essentially due to two kinds of factors: imbalance in public support levels between Europe and the US, and Europe's own industrial structure and working methods.

Direct and indirect support from the US government to its industry impacts both on the industry's technological level and on its costs, through, among other factors, economies of scale in manufacturing. The latter, related to the manufacturing process and, especially, to non-recurring costs, are seen as perhaps the greatest advantage to the US players. For example, today's most successful commercial satellite platform benefited from an initial US Navy order of 10 units. Since then, more than 50 have been ordered by commercial operators. By comparison, the most successful European platforms have not exceeded 10 -15 orders. It has been estimated that, in the past five years, government funding of the US satellite communications industry (through procurement and RTD for civilian and military programmes) amounted to ECU 9 billions, while commercial sales represented

only 26% of the industry's revenue. The corresponding figures for Europe are respectively ECU 2 billions and 45%. Although this latter share indicates a good performance of the European industry, the absolute figures highlight the disproportion between the levels of US and European public funding in this industry.

Turnover by market (MECU)

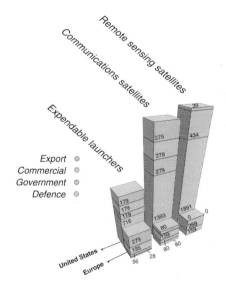

6 See the Commission's "Green Paper on Innovation" of December 1995

Given this disproportion, it is vital that all available funding in Europe, whether civilian or military, at national or European level, is used in the most effective way in order to render industry more competitive. ESA will remain an important actor and its ongoing reflection on industrial policy and the application of geographic return is to be welcome. The current system, originally designed to help the birth of a new European industry, could now be improved by stressing economic efficiency mechanisms and the objective of world competitiveness in the market-oriented space domains.

The industry's structure, characterised by considerable fragmentation and overlapping of competence both at prime and subcontractor level, also puts it at a cost disadvantage with respect to their American competitors who, moreover, benefit from a mature domestic market and a much higher volume of government contracts. It is difficult for the Europeans to offset that disadvantage through e.g. superior R&D, marketing, or other factors. The fragmentation of the European industry is also a problem when it comes to facing the risks (financial, commercial, technical) inherent to the new satellite systems being proposed at global scale.

The overall international scenario affecting space is evolving at a great speed creating new perspectives for the use of space; in the context of the emerging Information Society, the markets for space applications are developing fast, particularly in the areas of telecommunications and navigation, while Earth Observation is emerging from the realm of science towards an increased role of the market. Simultaneously, world competition on the markets for satellites and launch services is becoming increasingly intense and global.

The relevant European Union instruments (including regulatory actions) should be used in order to create the harmonised environment appropriate to facilitating investment and in order to support more efficient industrial structures, encouraging the upgrading of the European space industry in terms of competitiveness and quality.

The relations between this complex web of industrial players, and their working methods, remain largely influenced by space agency programmes, more than by the needs of the users. Indeed, a commercial customer purchasing a satellite system has to consider a number of factors, beside price and technological performance. Delivery times, financing, insurance and associated services are all elements in a complex package that it is increasingly necessary for space manufacturers to offer with their products.

The European space industry has, in the past few years, been improving its approach to customers along those lines. It has also taken significant steps towards consolidation and streamlining of its structures, through agreements or mergers, although these actions do not yet appear sufficient when compared to the impressive steps taken in the US industry.

Another characteristic of the European industrial fabric is a relatively low level of vertical integration, especially towards the downstream services and equipment markets. This is not to say that vertical integration constitutes the only model to follow. Innovative forms of cooperation between industry and operators are needed, if European initiatives are to emerge in response to the American ones.

In any case, it is clear that business and profitability are shifting downstream (towards network user equipment and services) conferring a strategic advantage to vertically integrated companies, especially in the new global telecommunications landscape. A greater part of the space telecommunications market will also be taken up by consortia where the satellite maker is a strategic partner, or is integrated in a wider group promoting the project. This has to be born in mind in a context where the opportunities open to independent manufacturers may not be expanding much.

Specialisation, on the other hand, also has its benefits, especially for the industry of smaller countries. Small and medium enterprises (SMEs) are generally recognised to be the main source of new jobs in all Member States. In fact research work has shown that a small proportion of about 4% of enterprises contribute for some 50% of all net job creation. SMEs throughout Europe already play a role in the space and downstream sectors, such as remote sensing data services. Particular attention has to paid to their positioning in the evolving context, and full use will be made of the Commission actions for the improvement of the business environment and the promotion of the development of these enterprises.

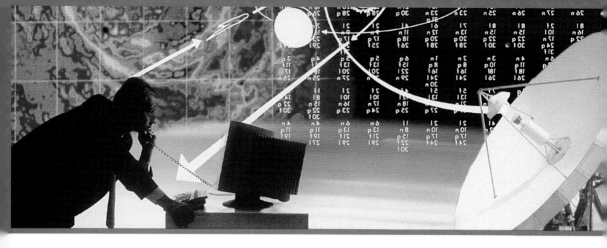

ROLE OF THE EUROPEAN ACTORS

As pointed out market-oriented applications are a growing but still not the dominant component of space activity. Their share is about 30% in Europe, but only 10% or less in the case of the other main space powers. Governments, through their space programmes and a number of other means, have an important impact in this sector and influence the nature of the game being played in the commercial arena. This highlights the importance of a strategic concertation of all European actors involved.

ESA should remain one central piece of the institutional scheme, fostering European cooperation and strategic planning in the space field. Together with national space agencies, it should reinforce the European technological base and remain a mainstay of European industry, through the design and implementation of space programmes for their specific objectives.

The European states, which have fostered the emergence of this industry through ESA and their space programmes, should now recognise that the context has evolved and that a more European, market-oriented approach is needed, where industry and service providers play a more active role. Failing that, no actions at EU or any other level can ensure the survival of this industry on a sound economic basis.

The partners in the development of space technologies and applications in the European Union

- The European Community: support to the development of the market, pilot and demonstration projects, methodological research ...

- The governements of the European States and their space agencies or national programmes: development of the space segmentl, exploratory and application missions, launching facilities ...

- The European Space Agency: development of the space segment, "Explorer" and "Earth watch" missions, launchers ...

- The Space Industry: prime and sub-contractorsfor the space and ground segments, value added companies for services and products.

- The Space system operators such as:

  - EUMETSAT for meteorology,

  - EUTELSAT for telecommunications

  - EUROCONTROL for air traffic management.

- The end users

Industry should be free to elaborate its strategy and choose a path, towards restructuring, which is adapted to the European framework. Issues such as industry consolidation, vertical integration and international cooperation are vital to the industry's global competitiveness. These issues have to be considered by taking into account European competition rules as well as the global challenges posed by the US and other competitors.

The Commission will work towards an open and competitive environment as the basis for a strong European industry and is willing to assist in the analysis of innovative strategic industrial alliances, contributing to a progressive awareness of the common European interests. It will also use its competence to ensure a level playing field within Europe and beyond. Furthermore, the Union is active in several policy fields mentioned above, for which space applications can be of strategic importance, and therefore has a stake in the development of those applications.

Its role must be seen within the subsidiarity principle, and in particular:

○ the need to improve coordination of European RTD and industrial policies, in a context where competition is global and Europe does not have in general a strong position.

○ the European-wide or global reach of space applications, which leaves little scope for national solutions.

○ the international coordination issues pertaining to those applications (orbital slots, frequencies, licensing, standardisation) where the lack of a common European voice constitutes a serious handicap to a strong market position.

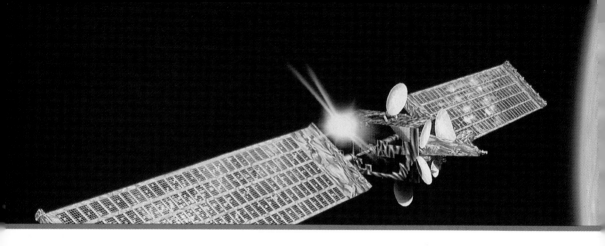

SPACE TELECOMMUNICATIONS

Telecommunication is by far the most widespread application of space technology, with 75% of all satellites at present being communications satellites. For the decade ahead (1996-2005), the world market corresponding solely to satellites for fixed communications and broadcasting is conservatively estimated at ECU 12-16 billions, launchings at ECU 9-10 billions, with operator revenues ECU 30-40 billions.

The estimated ground station and terminal market is ECU 50-70 billions and for end-user services, ECU 120-160 billions. Current services provided in Europe cover namely voice and mobile telecommunications, high speed data, and increasingly business communications to small traffic terminals (VSAT).

Since the last Communication by the Commission on space policy in 1992, there has been a resurgence of interest in the use of satellite communications prompted by technological developments which have enabled satellite systems to become a major mode of distribution of home entertainment television, and to compete with other communication technologies for new markets for mobile and very broadband communications. There is today a 'business synergy' to be developed between modern satellite systems and basic terrestrial infrastructure, and a convergence between the 'direct to home' of satellite television and the 'direct to user' of satellite business communications.

R&D and system aspects of space communications

USA budget

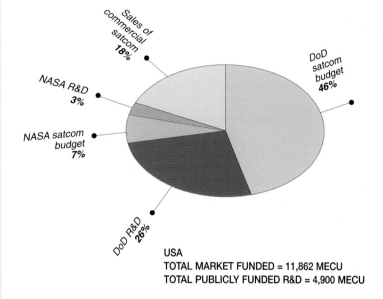

USA
TOTAL MARKET FUNDED = 11,862 MECU
TOTAL PUBLICLY FUNDED R&D = 4,900 MECU

EUROPE budget

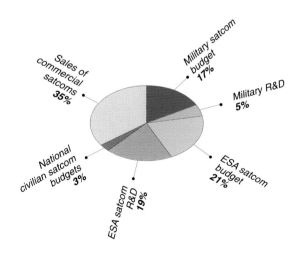

Relative size of Europe/USA budgets from 1990 to 1994
Source: European Commission (1995)

EUROPE
TOTAL MARKET = 3,712 MECU
TOTAL PUBLICLY FUNDED R&D = 1,304 MECU

Two promising new markets present challenges for European industry; when mature, each should provide industrial and service elements of economic size comparable to that of today's fixed satellite communications systems. They are:

○ satellite personal communications systems (satellite-PCS), mobile communications for handheld GSM type terminals and voice/data services, one of which has extensive participation of European space industry. Each proposed system is targeting 1 to 2 million users worldwide;

○ very broadband digital communication systems. These systems are based on global satellite constellations and are intended to serve the explosive demand for Internet type data, voice and interactive multimedia services as a major building block of the Global Information Infrastructure.

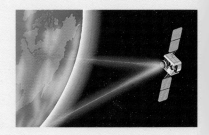

Proposed actions

The Commission proposes to enhance the role of satellite communications. This will be done in cooperation with ESA, national agencies and Member States, by developing a coherent set of policies and actions along three main lines: regulatory framework, external policy and RTD.

Advanced technologies for the development of global broadband digital satellite systems (for fixed or mobile applications) have been developed over the last few years through ESA or national agency programmes. Such programmes are primarily concentrating on payload technologies and to a lesser extent, on ground segment technologies. On the other hand, Union supported programmes are concentrating more on technology and systems developments for ground segment and applications. Thus, European Union RTD Framework Programmes and national and ESA programmes should play complementary roles in promoting the commercialisation of space telecommunications services to address the new passive markets for communications and multimedia services, including Internet broadband access systems.

In relation to telecommunications, the full liberalisation of services, an open access to space segment and a balanced access to satellite markets should be pursued in WTO; a harmonised regulatory regime for the introduction of satellite PCS services in Europe has to be consolidated, in conjunction with member States; the concertation of European positions in international fora, in particular on the allocations of frequency spectrum and orbital allocations, has to be increased; a specific Action Plan on key issues for satellite communications addressing in particular issues of the regulatory framework, the strengthening of efforts at European level in international fora, and research and development aspects will be proposed by the Commission.

In the field of mobile communications, research is today primarily centred around the development of the GSM follow up, also called UMTS (Universal Mobile Telephony Service). In Europe, the 4th Framework Programme provides a major source of funding through its ACTS component.

There will be a need to continue the integration effort, in such a way that European industry is in a good position to provide terminals for next generation mobile networks, with both terrestrial and satellite communications capabilities, thus maintaining the leading position obtained with GSM.

Advanced broadband digital communications satellite systems are now being planned to provide communications infrastructure to support the Global Information Society, based on constellations of satellites in either geostationary or non-geostationary orbit, and optimised to serve the demand for Internet-type data, voice, and interactive multimedia services.Whilst initially almost all these initiatives came from the US, both European industry and operators are now beginning to compete with their own projects and plans.

On 10 October 1996, an informal High Level meeting took place between the Commission, EU ministers, and industry representatives to discuss the need for specific action in the satellite communications sector. As a result of this meeting the Commission has announced in the Telecommunications Council of November 28, 1996, that, as part of its commitment of a partnership between public and private sector players, it will present a coherent approach to both R&D and regulatory/policy matters for the satellite communications sector addressed in the form of an Action Plan to be submitted to Council in 1997. This Action Plan will be in full coherence with this present Communication and its objective shall be:

○ to present a framework in which private and public partners cooperate,

○ to stimulate the satellite sector to take initiatives and lead the public sector actors

○ to propose concrete actions in order to advance in broadband multimedia via satellite and in personal communications

○ to reinforce the international position both at policy and industrial level. In particular, the concertation of European positions on the allocation of frequency spectrum and orbital allocations has to be increased in international fora;

○ to review the satellite communications aspects in the Community R&D programme, with a view to increase its relative position

○ to reinforce the cooperation with ESA, and with CEPT.

SATELLITE
NAVIGATION AND POSITIONING

Satellite positioning systems (GPS and GLONASS[7]) have been deployed for military purposes by the US and Russia. Non-encrypted signals from these systems are available free of charge for civilian use, which has opened up a market for navigation equipment, increasingly used in all modes of transport, and for positioning equipment used in a wide range of other applications. Satellite navigation and positioning systems are thus evolving from a primarily military to a wider civilian use.

Several studies underline the prospective benefits of satellite navigation all over the world. The advantages to be gained over existing systems include simplification through the use of a single system which could meet all users requirements operating world-wide 24 hours/day. A space based system will also provide improved accuracy of position and velocity measurement which will lead in turn to a reduction of waiting times, fuel savings, better environmental protection and a reduction in the number of accidents: the estimated savings are about 20 bn ECU/year world-wide. Such considerations have led both the International Civil Aviation Organisation (ICAO) and the International Maritime Organisation (IMO) to adopt space based systems as key components of the next generation of navigation and positioning services.

---

7 GPS: Global Positioning System, GLONASS: Global navigation System

Apart from the social and economic benefits one has also to consider the industrial opportunities. Since satellites have only a limited lifetime, space segments must be continuously maintained and updated. Ground segments must be extended to provide greater geographical coverage and improved services. Both must be supplied by industry. The market for user equipment already amounted to MECU 477 in 1994, and is predicted to rise to ECU 4 billions in 2000 and ECU 25 billions in 2005. A market of comparable size is also developing for peripheral services and hardware units.

Experience shows that only those nations and industries with a decisive influence on the system infrastructure will remain competitive in the market. The objective of the European Union is to raise European industry to a level of competitiveness enabling it to participate in the deployment of a Global Navigation Satellite System (GNSS), in the definition of interoperability requirements and industrial standards, thereby giving industry the opportunity for an early entry in the market.

Satellite navigation market

Sales in millions $

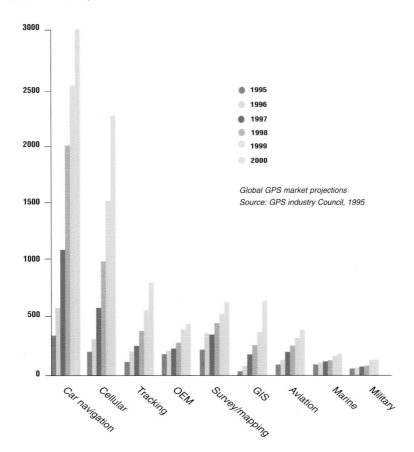

- 1995
- 1996
- 1997
- 1998
- 1999
- 2000

Global GPS market projections
Source: GPS industry Council, 1995

The free availability of the signals and the political complications due to the dual use character of today's systems, however, make it very difficult for a purely private initiative to open the door to Europe's full participation in this market, and only a government-industry partnership has a chance to provide a breakthrough. Although aviation represents only a limited share of the total market, its key role is due to the fact that no other sector has such strict requirements. The present GPS system, under the control of one single country, has some weak points: accuracy is insufficient; geographical coverage is not total; the technical failure probability is too high for safety critical applications; warning times in case of system failures are too long. Due to these shortcomings, public authorities all over the world have started to commission GPS augmentations, in order to provide better integrity, availability and accuracy to services for civilian use. This network of systems currently emerging around GPS and possibly GLONASS will become a seamless, worldwide augmentation system for air navigation.

The Commission[8], Council[9] and the European Parliament[10] have recognised the need for Europe to play a key role for the implementation of GNSS and adopted a two-track approach:

○ A European augmentation to the existing military Constellation GPS and GLONASS in order to meet the civilian users requirements (GNSS-1) and at the same time,

○ Preparatory work for the design and organisation of the second generation system (GNSS-2).

The Commission has also set up a High Level Group consisting of representatives from national governments, users, industry, relevant industrial organisations and potential service providers which assists the Commission in the development of an Action Plan for deployment of GNSS.

To co-ordinate the European Contribution to GNSS-1 and initiate actions on GNSS-2 the European Community with ESA and EUROCONTROL have gathered their efforts within the European Tripartite Group (ETG). The Community provides the political support and complementary financial support for projects through its Trans-European Transport Networks policy and its telematics and transport RTD programmes. ESA implements the ground segment and will operate the European Geostationary Navigation Overlay System (EGNOS) until it reaches the Advanced Operational Capability (AOC) phase. When AOC has been completed, EGNOS can be approved as a primary means of navigation. EUROCONTROL defines the Civil Aviation requirements and will validate the system in accordance with those requirements.

More specifically, the Commission is supporting the following actions:

○ From the Telematics applications programme of the Fourth Framework Programme, and concerning GNSS-1, several projects address the development of on-board receivers and demonstrate the ability of local area augmentation systems for air, sea and rail applications. At the same time, preparatory work has been launched which will identify the operational and functional requirements for a GNSS system, encompassing both GNSS-1 and GNSS-2.

○ From the Transport research programme, concerning the potential benefits of the application of satellite-based services, a project assesses the transport policy requirements for the integration of information, communication and navigation technologies.

○ Within the Trans-European Transport Network actions, support has been given to provision of access to the Inmarsat III navigation payloads; a Council decision has been adopted which provides guidelines for the implementation of a Trans-european Navigation and Positioning Network[11].

Within the framework of the Common Transport Policy, a baseline European Radionavigation Plan (ERNP) is currently being developed, taking into account the requirements of international bodies (IMO, ICAO, ITU). The ERNP will help in the rationalisation and harmonisation of European policies concerning radio-navigation systems facilitating among others the introduction of satellite based services. Studies are being launched, one of them is to analyse the costs and benefits of a contribution to GNSS. This study shall analyse in particular the benefits to users from the various sectors. Another study is to design an international system and determine the nature and thoroughly analyse the approach to a future system.

Position determination by satellite may be used in surveillance systems and therefore in the monitoring of the implementation of Commission policies. As an example, the Commission is preparing a proposal for a Council regulation on the establishment of a satellite vessel monitoring system for the control of the Union Fisheries Policy.

8   Communication on the Satellite Navigation Services. COM(94)248 of June 1994

9   Council Resolution 94/c379/02 of 19.02.94

10   E.P. Resolution 209.909 final of 30.11.94

11   Decision 1692/96/EC of 23/7/96 O.J. L 228

Proposed Actions

With the assistance of the High Level Group, the Action Plan will be drawn up to cover:

○ Proposals for institutional arrangements to facilitate the channelling of investments, placing of contracts and solving of ownership problems. Extending the remit of an existing agency or the creation of a new body are two of the options under consideration to ensure the provision of the appropriate infrastructure which will satisfy the certification requirements.

○ Definition of a legal and regulatory framework with provision for different operators to provide navigation and positioning services to specific users.

○ Definition of the configuration and implementation schedule for Full Operational Capability (FOC) which provides fail safe operation needed for safety critical operation by providing redundancy in ground and space segments.

○ Identification of funding options for the deployment of FOC to start not later than 1999.

○ Agreements with other countries or regions who have no space segment but wish to offer satellite navigation services over their territory and are willing to contribute to the required extensions to EGNOS. African countries, the Indian Ocean region, South America, Eastern Europe and the countries of the former Soviet Union have already expressed interest.

This work will be carried out under a co-operation framework aimed at meeting global interoperability requirements and the requirements of international conventions.

As regards navigation and positioning services by satellite, Europe should play a key role by its participation to the development of a global system answering the needs of civil society;

A specific action plan under preparation, will be presented by the Commission.

Due to public investment amounting to ECU 10 bn for the supply of GPS, backed up by substantial orders for military terminals, the US has dominated the satellite navigation market. This experience has been used to draw up de facto standards in national bodies and are already being used to construct equipment. There is a danger that these will be adopted as international standards under pressure from current users. Urgent action is needed to strengthen the European standardisation process with a view to adopting a common European Position in critical areas. The global objective should be to discuss regional

standards between Europe and the US before discussion within international bodies.

Certification of a space system issues new challenges to regulators especially those responsible for safety of life level services. Relevant authorities must decide on their certification policy for GNSS1 which depends ultimately on a system or systems (GPS, GLONASS) which are under the ultimate control of the military authorities of the US and Russia. In consequence, deployment of a European specific contribution to GNSS-2 offers the appropriate way for Europe to maintain its sovereignty in the area of satellite navigation.

Although GNSS-2-related developments have been initiated in Europe these are on too small a scale to provide realistic competition and the following urgent actions are needed:

○ Speedy approval of the Action Plan, especially the institutional arrangements.

○ Support for industry to develop user segment equipment particularly for land applications.

○ Initiation of work for the design, development and organisation of GNSS-2, adding to the preparatory work already done under the Fourth Framework Programme and under ARTES 9 by ESA, leading to an in orbit demonstration of industry's capability to supply the system. Support of relevant actions in the Fifth Framework Programme in close cooperation with ESA and national agencies.

To speed up the process, the possibility must also be considered of a European dedicated navigation payload, which may be launched in combination with another system including services other than navigation.

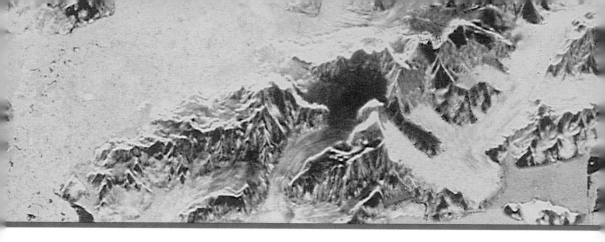

EARTH
OBSERVATION FROM SPACE

In the last 25 years, Europe, thanks to ESA and national Space agencies programmes, has established a sound base in satellite observation of the Earth with the SPOT, ERS and METEOSAT series which has to be exploited to the full. As regards meteorological satellites, for example, EUMETSAT operates systems meeting the needs of European States and contributes to a global meteorological system providing services throughout the world.

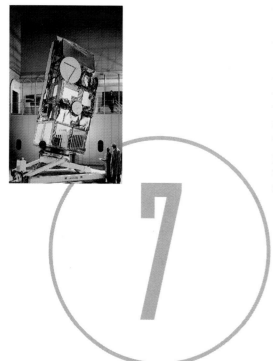

The world market for civil remote sensing, in the decade ahead, is estimated at a minimum of ECU 12 billions for satellites and the corresponding launches, ECU 1.2 billions for data sales, ECU 4 billions for terrestrial receiving and processing equipment and more than ECU 12 billions for services related to value-added products and services. According to recent estimations the whole market for data and related services (excluding meteorology) would be about 270 MECU for Europe in 2000. So far, the customers are mainly public entities. Not only must potential clients be shown that the data supply is cost effective for their application, but also that the data can be delivered reliably, in good time, and for the foreseeable future.

Given the limited revenue from sales, the value added industry has been unable until now to invest in attracting new customers. Although the potential is promising, the European market in data from satellite observation of the Earth is still largely underdeveloped and needs a major European effort to make it grow.

Given that the EU is amongst the largest purchasers of data services in Europe, it is uniquely placed to play a fundamental role in developing this market, both as a pioneer customer and by supporting the development of data derived information services. This was indeed advocated by industry, which specifically recommended a "two step approach" as a phased means of establishing self sustaining markets. This constitutes a way to ensure the continuity of service, given a regular and adequate provision of new systems, which is the responsibility of industry and other organisations. In the longer term, once the market is consolidated, it will be industry's role to deliver data services to customers on a commercial basis.

However, industry will be able to do this only if it has clear indications as to the market stability and size. Here the Commission could provide a significant contribution by accurately expressing Europe's requirements for Earth observation and corresponding services with a related estimate of the annual value of those services, this expression being divorced from any perception of the ability, or otherwise, of Earth observation technology to supply those services. On the basis of this assessment, the challenge to Industry will be to improve the quality, timeliness and cost of those services whilst developing a profitable business. Industry needs also appropriate financial engineering instruments enabling it to take the risks associated with the development of any new advanced technologies.

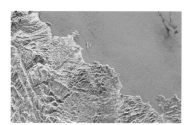

An important step in the direction of further developing the field was the joint document by ESA, EUMETSAT and the European Commission[12] presented to the Council of ESA in Toulouse on 20 October 1995 concerning a European policy on Earth observation by satellite which has the following main objectives:

○ satisfy user needs on a permanent basis, mainly by establishing operational satellite services, ensuring continuous supply of data and services, and maintaining a state of the art configuration;

○ stimulate industrial profitability and competitiveness by promoting the widest possible market (including military) and reducing the cost of satellite observation systems to a minimum to ensure that they are used to the full;

○ achieve strategic objectives, ensuring guaranteed access to data where essential to the security of Europe or to the preservation of its environment, maintaining and developing its capacity to enable it to play a global role.

---

12 *Proposal for a European policy for Earth observation from space ESA/PB-EO(95)7, rev. 2*

Earth observation at the service of the citizen

Satellites in low Earth orbit are repeatedly passing overhead, scanning the land and sea beneath them and transmitting the resulting data back to receiving stations on Earth.

Optical instruments are particularly valuable for viewing small details for the kind of applications that have been familiar since the start of aerial photography. Many inaccessible areas of the Earth's surface have now been mapped for the first time, with high precision, using information acquired by the SPOT series of satellites. By combining the information from several instruments European scientists and technicians have developed some truly remarkable systems for monitoring various themes. One outstanding achievement to illustrate such an approach has been provided by the JRC's MARS project to furnish its clients, particularly the DG VI and EUROSTAT, with some of the information they need to execute their mandates. Humanitarian organisations depend on these maps, which can be kept right up to date, to localise disasters and work out feasible approach routes. At the other end of the scale, some optical instruments are designed to collect data over huge swaths of the planet at a single sweep. In one application of such data, locust breeding grounds can be detected and teams of eradication experts brought in to stamp out the swarm before it can begin its devastating migration.

Instruments capable of measuring the surface brightness temperature are routinely used in semi-arid lands for detecting areas that are at risk of bush fire, and in temperate lands for mapping areas where orchards or spring crops have suffered from frost damage. In this way disasters may be prevented on the one hand, and farmers compensated for loss of their crops on the other. Over the oceans, such instruments can measure the temperature of the ocean skin, and the resulting maps can show where nutrient-rich cold water is upwelling from the depths, attracting planckton and shoals of fish. In colder waters, the deliveries of food around northern capes can be maintained for vital weeks longer by monitoring the approaching sea ice with such instruments.

Radar instruments, such as the Synthetic Aperture Radar on ESA's ERS satellites, are also constanly monitoring our planet from orbit. These instruments are essentially all-weather, and can image the planet's surface through cloud and at night. These instruments have proved themselves invaluable in measuring wave height and wind speeded to measuring the extent of floods, and in the future should become a vital element in the struggle to limit and prevent flooding.

Proposed actions

In order to reach those objectives, each of the partners involved has to determine the appropriate ways and means according to its own procedures. At the Union level, the Commission has already given impetus to this sector through a dedicated activity within the Fourth Framework Programme of RTD. The following actions are proposed for the near future:

On the basis of market studies involving the Commission's departments, national and european space agencies, and major industrial groups as potential promotors, the use of existing or planned European missions will be fostered. New application missions with sufficient potential return to attract investment by industry could be initiated with the Commission acting as pioneer customer in the first phase, with the support of space agencies. They will be implemented in full by such industrial investors or appropriate operational entities in the second phase with the aim of providing an operational service on a commercial basis.

The Union action will be targeted at a limited number of application areas related to the implementation of its various policies such as:

♀ **Monitoring of land use and resources:** Europe has already made a major effort in this domain and a high level of expertise has been reached which has to be valorized. Additional research will be undertaken and new operational techniques developed to improve and foster European capacities in this area. Demonstration and pilot projects will be implemented in the fields of agriculture, forest, urban planning, waste disposal, etc. in close cooperation with industrial partners as main users (agro-food companies, forest exploitation companies, public work enterprises, local collectivities, ...). Such projects will contribute to Union's initiatives towards sustainable management of environmental resources.

♀ **Monitoring of surface waters:** The experience gained at European level will be optimised and developed through demonstration and pilot projects based on existing missions, before launching new dedicated application missions in collaboration e.g. with water management companies. This action will form part of the initiative proposed by the Commission on water.

♀ **Monitoring of fisheries:** Earth observation techniques are already well developed and their potential for the management of fisheries will provide an important complement to satellite based vessel tracking systems and in situ measurements. Large fishing companies are amongst the main potential industrial partners as promoters.

Some of the application areas have a strategic and political interest for the Union involving other European or developing countries. On the basis of the know-how already acquired from the on-going or past European missions, new application missions, in particular ESA's "Earth watch missions" could be envisaged, notably in the following fields:

♀ **Monitoring of Coastal areas:** The strategic importance of those areas for the Community is obvious given the length and diversity of its coast line. The technologies and instruments developed to meet these needs will also have applications at world level in particular in the developing countries. Preliminary studies should be launched on the various coastal areas of Europe, taking account of their specific characteristics (Mediterranean Sea, Baltic Sea, North Sea and Atlantic arc). As a first step, the Commission proposes to identify the many initiatives under way, coordinate them and prepare, in close cooperation with the interested partners, a new strategic initiative to establish an information system on Mediterranean coastal areas using, amongst other sources of information, space remote sensing techniques.

♀ **Monitoring of major risks and natural hazards:** The Council of Europe, in cooperation with ESA and the Commission,. has initiated an action in this field and exploratory studies are currently under way, involving the countries of Central and Eastern Europe. This is an area where civil and military technologies are of interests for that particular use, and the dual application of these technologies may enable them to be exploited to the full. The Commission with the interested parties, in particular the civil security services, will identify and support pilot projects in order to pave the way for the implementation of new initiatives merging various space techniques in the fields of telecommunication, positioning, and remote sensing.

As part of the implementation of the EU environmental policy, the Commission will continue to support the development of applications of Earth observation techniques by carrying out projects for environmental monitoring, including those aimed at increasing the effectiveness of European environmental legislation and international environmental agreements. This will be done in cooperation with national environment agencies and the EEA. In complement to existing or planned missions, new missions could be envisaged with the support of space agencies, in particular ESA through its "Earth explorer missions" initiative, and other appropriate partners such as EUMETSAT, in order to provide continuous public services in the following fields:

• Ocean monitoring:

The experience so far gained should also be exploited at European level. In order to develop further operational oceanography systems and to meet the requirements of the Global Ocean Observing System (GOOS) and its European branch (EUROGOOS), the integration of data collected with other in situ observations could in particular be the subject of a European action.

• Atmosphere monitoring:

In this field, application of space techniques are, for the time being, limited to scientific research. Initially benefit will be drawn from existing missions in order to demonstrate the feasibility of the technique from an operational point of view. Future "explorer missions" could be envisaged in cooperation with ESA or EUMETSAT.

To reinforce the necessary scientific and technical base and promote the use of scientific results to develop operational applications, the Commission will continue to implement the Union RTD Framework programmes particularly as regards basic methodological research and pilot and demonstration projects of a pre-operational nature in the above areas and in other less advanced sectors.

An important contribution to the development of the market for Earth observation data-derived services could be given by the European Union through the implementation and operation of its policies;

methodological research and pilot projects will be proposed in dedicated areas of Community interest;

this sector should be progressively taken over in most cases by private investors and the Commission should facilitate this process;

the development of service organisations and new European operational entities designed to deliver space information services have to be stimulated;

discussions with EUMETSAT will be opened to explore its possible role in providing data for environmental monitoring;

measures in the field of education and training, as well as measures to promote international cooperation and development, have to be coordinated at the Union level in close cooperation with Member States and relevant organisations notably the International Space University in Strasbourg.

Work will be also carried out on applications and further development of sensors using advanced technology in collaboration with the appropriate partners taking into account the need of assuring continuity during the demonstration phase.

The Union's programme for a Centre for Earth Observation (CEO) has an important role to play in the above. Aimed at bringing together the users and suppliers of data, it will allow quicker and easier access to such data by promoting the development of common standards and formats. The CEO will also keep users better informed, enabling them to make full use of the processed information, while giving to the data providers the appropriate means and tools to satisfy the users needs. It will thus be an integral part of future operational systems.

The development of the market also involves the training and education of potential users, particularly those using Earth observation data services in the decision making process, including those of developing countries. The Commission will continue the action undertaken in collaboration with ESA, the space agencies in the Member States and at international level (such as the International Space University).

Where the need is perceived, and with the appropriate organisations, the Commission will foster the creation of new European operational entities. In particular, in the field of environmental monitoring, it will explore with EUMETSAT, and the partners concerned, the possibility of that body providing space data relevant to this field.

In order to foster the applications of Earth observation from Space, the Commission will continue to study legal aspects of the use of Earth observation data as well as the broad principles of a data policy in agreement with the opening of a commercial market. The question of the frequencies and orbital slots allocation will be also taken into consideration by the Commission in international negociations.

Finally, the Commission, jointly with his partners, will give further consideration to the establishment of a coherent European strategy to develop and implement operational systems for observing the Earth and its Environment. Such a strategy for coordinating systems already existing or planned at the European level without compromising their identities will give Europe the opportunity to make full and coherent contribution to the setting up of an Integrated Global Observing Strategy as proposed in the CEOS.

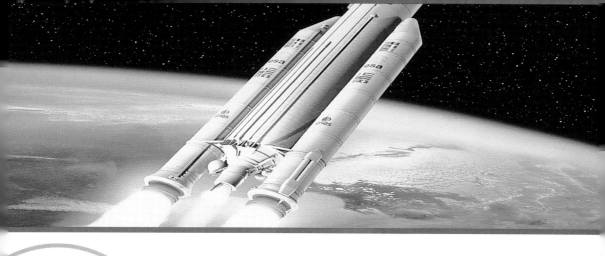

8 SPACE LAUNCH SERVICES

The need for Europe to secure an independent capability to provide applications satellite systems, be they for telecommunications, television or Earth observation, was a key political driver in the original decision in the early 70s to undertake the Ariane programme. This political commitment, which furthermore achieved for Europe a leadership position in the commercial market for space launch services, largely paying back the Member States' investment, is still valid today and remains a pre-condition for the continued access of Europe to space and space applications.

Europe's leadership position in the commercial market for space launch services needs to be maintained against increasing competition, characterised by the presence of advanced versions of existing US launchers, and the entry into the market of vehicles from Russia, Ukraine, and China. This considerable increase in the supply of space launch services, and, in certain cases, at extremely low prices, threatens to destabilise the market.

A fundamental condition for the maintenance and further development of European space launch services is a degree of market access similar to that offered in the EU and the existence of fair trading conditions. As regards market access, the objective should be not only to ensure that there are no restrictions for space launch services provided for civilian uses, but also that there are no nationality conditions attached to space launch services provided to governmental entities. The latter are very frequent in countries such as China and the USA, whereas the EU has an open market.

A framework of international rules designed to secure fair competition in the space launcher market has to be established;

the range of launch vehicles available, adapted to new market requirements, might be broadened.

This should be adressed primarily in WTO, where the GATT covers space launch services. The Commission and the European industry are convinced that it should be in Europe's interest to start exploring the possibility to discuss and establish basic rules ("Rules of the Road") for the conduct of open and fair competition among the most important space launch service providers. This should include the issues of public support to this industry as well as balanced access to each country's domestic market.

Such negotiations should include the US, whose industry benefits from an extraordinary and unequalled level of governmental support and military programmes, as well as emerging suppliers like Russia, Ukraine and China. A particular aim would be to give an important neighbour like Russia the chance of a smooth and progressive integration into the market for commercial space launch services on a fair and balanced basis.

The Commission will work actively with Member States in order to arrive at a common long term strategy in this sector and reach a practical solution for the conduct of international negotiations. This focus on a forward looking international strategy aimed at opening markets, exploiting new opportunities and creating fair trading conditions, implies that market opening agreements would render redundant market sharing ones.

The rapid growth in proposals for communications satellites for satellite personal systems and for broadband communications using non-geostationary orbits (LEOs, MEOs) leads to a broadened requirement for launch services over that of the basic market for satellites in the geostationary orbit. The Commission regards the continued presence of European industry in the provision of launch services as essential, and encourages the competent space agencies and industry to consider how best to maintain a comprehensive European offer over the whole spectrum of launch vehicle services.

DEFENCE AND DUAL USE
SPACE TECHNOLOGIES

Although it is not within the Commission's remit to consider the military aspects of space technology applications, any European strategy should ensure the convergence of civil and military effort in order to avoid duplications and make the best use of the available public funding. The relatively high cost of space systems make them a first choice candidate for European cooperation, since individual countries will have difficulty reaching the critical mass to justify such an investment.

**The Commission
encourages a coordinated
approach by the European
Union, the Member States, the
WEU and ESA towards dual-use
space technologies.**

Space technology is of central and growing importance for many types of military missions in the fields of telecommunications, navigation, intelligence, early warning and meteorology. Initially, military needs have driven space technology, which was channelled to civilian applications at an ulterior stage. More recently, the situation has changed in that civilian applications are driving the market and justifying themselves the technological investments.

The degree of technological commonality between military and civilian space systems is in general high, although it varies from one application to the next. Launch systems and propulsion also benefit from important spill overs between the military and civilian sectors. The US industry has long benefited from such spillovers in the commercial markets, thanks to a military space budget which is over forty times Europe's.

As stressed in its Communication on the defence industries[13], strong and competent industrial bases hold the key to Europe's independence and hence any common effort contributing to the strengthening of these capacities must be welcomed and stimulated.

---

13   COM (96) 10 final

INTERNATIONAL COOPERATION

Since the removal of East-West barriers, international cooperation and exchanges in space programmes have flourished in previously impossible ways, a trend encouraged by budgetary restrictions and the realisation of common interests. At the same time, in the private sector, international risk sharing in the new information and multimedia industries is fostering the access to new markets, by bringing together industry and a number of different actors.

Europe must be a key player in these international partnerships, provided that they are balanced. This implies that Europe must keep or acquire a critical mass, at least in the fields where this is not yet true, in order to draw full benefit from international cooperation with its large economic partners. This situation also implies a coordinated approach to problems at European level, and the appropriate concertation structures.

In this perspective, the opportunities for industrial and technological cooperation with established players such as the US, Russia, China and Japan, but also the emerging ones such as India and Brazil, must be considered.

International cooperation is also needed in the field of space debris and the Commission could give a contribution to the already on-going works in various instances (UN, ESA).

International cooperation in space technologies may enable certain objectives of the Union to be met, as regards third countries. The countries of Eastern Europe should benefit from an early integration in trans-European networks, and therefore should be associated to the European initiatives such as those in satellite communications and satellite navigation.

Some of the countries from the former Soviet Union could also be partners in space relevant projects. Within the framework of its economic cooperation with the New Independent States (NIS) the Commission will continue to provide under the TACIS programme technical assistance to the aerospace industry. Through the International Science and Technology Centre in Moscow it will finance scientific cooperation with a view to integrating the scientific potential of the NIS into the global scientific community.

As for the developing countries, such as in the Mediterranean basin, space technologies can provide some pertinent solutions. Some of the possibilities were highlighted during a workshop on the construction of the Euro-Mediterranean Information Society - regulation framework and Developement of Communication Networks for Economic Cooperation (Palermo, 6/7 May 1996). In the light of the needs, the Union can take action under several of its mandates, whether they relate to RTD, development aid or economic cooperation. Depending on their level of technical maturity, the implementation of these space-derived solutions necessitates a considerable concertation effort, which the Commission proposes to undertake together with the developing countries and the partners concerned (agencies, industries, etc.) with the support of the appropriate Union instruments.

STANDARDISATION

The space industry has to cope with very stringent requirements in terms of quality and reliability. In Europe as elsewhere, the need to standardise products and procedures in this field has long been recognised. If anything, Europe's complex industrial structure makes such a need more pressing. Following a number of past attempts, the European Cooperation for Space Standardisation (ECSS) has now managed to put together a group of agencies and industry players which offer no doubt as to their European representativeness. Their programme aims at a comprehensive and coherent system of standards, based on a commercially-oriented strategy.

In order to foster the competitiveness of European industry, the Commission has given a mandate to ECSS and the European standards organisations CEN, CENELEC, and ETSI, inviting them to agree an cooperation arrangements and to elaborate an overall standardization strategy, identifying areas where standardization activities are to be carried out at the European level and at international level and identifying those specifications which should become formal standards and those which should remain within the exclusive sphere of ECSS.

FINANCING

Space projects, and in particular those corresponding to the new applications, require substantial up front investments with long pay-back periods. These projects are therefore very sensitive to the conditions in which funding can be obtained, as much as they are to manufacturing costs and market conditions, whilst European players have had to cope with the exchange risk associated with the fluctuations of the US dollar.

Space is generally associated with an image of high-risk technologies, with new applications in unproven yet potentially very competitive markets. However, this situation is evolving, with investor attitudes becoming more positive. New systems such as satellite PCS are offering "franchising" opportunities for rights to offer services in specific regions against equity investment in the system costs. To the extent that the European environment is perceived as an obstacle to the financing of similar initiatives in Europe, the EU can play a direct and indirect role in improving this situation.

Directly, the Commission will seek to identify and support projects of European interest in the fields of telecommunications, navigation control and Earth observation. These projects, on which all European partners should cooperate, will in principle be based on already existing or planned programmes of the Member States, ESA or national space agencies.

Innovative funding and guarantee mechanisms, including those of the European Investment Bank and European Investment Fund, should be used to facilitate the financing of commercial space projects.

Among other things they should use the resources of the RTD Framework Programme. Other resources could be made available under the framework of Trans European Networks, or, in accordance with the appropriate procedures, making use of the structural funds, agricultural development or cooperation budgets. It is worth noting, however, that the relevant parts of the Framework Programme as well as other instruments are severely constrained, and can at best provide a useful complement to the projects in question.

Initially, there should be no need for additional funding over and above existing levels and it should be a question above all of reallocating available funds among the topics selected as having a European interest, and achieving greater complementarity and synergy of work. Future needs will be determined on the basis of exploratory studies to be carried out in connection with specific selected projects. At the same time, the private sector should be called to take more responsibility in the implementation of these projects and to develop the appropriate infrastructures with the support of the public authorities.

Indirectly, the EU can give a major contribution to improving investment conditions, first of all by reducing the uncertainty which arises from the regulatory environment, trade policy regimes, etc. Initiatives from the Commission in promoting innovation or supporting SMEs could also pave the way to complement and facilitate the decision of the potential partners, financial entities, operators and users, to take risks in space-based commercial ventures.

The Union's contribution as a pioneer customer or demonstrator of space applications will also help service providers secure further private finance for space missions. In the context of Earth Observation, this has been described as a "two-step approach" to the development of a self-sustained industry.

The European Investment Bank (EIB), from 1990 to date, has provided resources worth more than ECU 1.5 billion for the funding of 15 European satellite communications projects. The Commission proposes to pursue and activate discussions with the EIB and the European Investment Fund to define appropriate ways and means to facilitate access to their respective funding mechanisms.

INSTITUTIONAL ASPECTS

It is necessary to implement or improve structures of collaboration and cooperation to reinforce the synergy of the European space effort at Member State and international level, maximising the return on the investment made, and ensuring respect for the individual responsibilities of the various partners in developing a coherent overall strategy. These structures should develop a sound relationship between Union bodies, national and European space agencies, industry, users, and other relevant scientific or operational entities. In order to improve complementarity of RTD activities, recourse to art 130K and L could be envisaged by the Commission.

The role of the Space Advisory Group set up in 1993 to provide a forum for discussing the broad lines of Union action in the space field will be strengthened to allow coordination and concertation of actions carried out at national or Union level.

Cooperation between the Commission and the European Space Agency, ESA, which currently has observer status at the Space Advisory Group, will be improved under the basis of Article 130M of the Treaty, respecting the independent status of this Agency, and under a negotiating mandate to be requested from the Council.

On the basis of Art. 228 of the Treaty, the Commission is proposing moreover to put in place appropriate structures for the management of specific projects selected in agreement with the partners concerned and with the involvement of users (the tripartite group EC/ESA/EUROCONTROL set up for the GNSS-1 project is an example for consideration). For example the Community, jointly with its partners, is promoting the development of an European Economic Interest Grouping (EEIG) to carry out such projects.

In the trade policy area, in order to ensure fair competition with third countries in the commercial market for space launch services, the Commission and Member States must find an institutional compromise for the conduct of inter-national negotiations. The Commission will continue to search for a rapid and practical solution and encourages the Member States to be forthcoming on this issue.

conclusions

This Communication highlights the urgent need for action in order to establish an appropriate environment for the development of applications of space techniques and to improve the competitiveness of European industry at world level.

Proposals in the above fields will be made by the Commission within the current and future RDT Framework Programmes with the key goal of consolidating the European satellite based infrastructure; certain activities could necessitate the use of other forms of Community support according to the particular modalities concerned, concrete measures will be taken by the Commission.

All these initiatives should be coordinated with those of Member States and of the European Space Agency in order to obtain, within European Union rules, the maximum degree of flexibility and synergy at the European level; the Commission, together with the European Space Agency and other organisations concerned, will take the necessary steps to this end; the Commission will continue to rely on the advice of the Space Advisory Group (SAG) and other advisory groups and to maintain regular dialogue with industrialists and users.

The Council of the European Union

The Council of the European Union welcomes the Commission's Communication "The European Union and Space" and recognizes the growing need to optimize Europe's investment in space by seeking synergies between EU policies and relevant European agencies, such as the European Space Agency (ESA), the programmes and projects of the Member States, and industries, including SMEs.

The Council encourages the Commission to continue and reinforce an active and dynamic dialogue with the Space sector (e.g. satellites, launchers, applications and services, including the ground segment) to take into consideration their concerns in the development of the different Community policies related to Space and its applications, in order to provide both support and guidance for coordinated development, recognising its own role as a customer for space-related services.

The Council welcomes the Commission's initiative to elaborate, in close consultation with the Member States, ESA and national space agencies, industry, users, operators and service providers, concrete action plans for the main areas of Space technology applications, in the sectors of telecommunications, navigation, earth observation and environmental monitoring, which should help provide focus and orientation for developing a European perspective in these areas for the benefit of industry and public as well as private users.

The Council recognizes that Community Research and Development policy, as laid down in the Framework Programmes, provides an important framework for support and synergies for space applications; considers therefore that ongoing Research and Development efforts relating to space, including, where appropriate, the future use of the International Space Station, should be taken into account in the development of the Fifth Framework Programme. It particularly encourages the Commission to coordinate the space activities of the Framework Programme with each other and with those action plans. Other support and guidance can be derived through a number of other policies, e.g. those relating to telecommunications, transport, environment, trade, international relations and development cooperation.

The Council calls upon the Commission to assure internal coordination of these activities; to work in close consultation with the Member States, in particular through the Space Advisory Group; to strengthen cooperation and coordination with ESA and to consult other bodies as appropriate, in order to facilitate, inter alia, the drawing up of common standards and procedures and the establishment of international rules to guarantee conditions for balanced competition in the market of space services.

The Council requests the Commission to report on the progress of its work before the end of 1998.

GLOSSARY

ACTS	Advanced Communications Technologies and Services
AOC	Advance Operational Capability
ARTES	Advanced Research and Telecommunication Systems
CEN	Comité Européen de Normalisation
CENELEC	Comité Européen de Normalisation Electrotechnique
CEO	Centre of Earth Observation
CEOS	Committee on Earth Observation Satellites
CEPT	Conférence Européenne des administrations des PTT
CNES	Centre National d'Etudes Spatiales
ECSS	European Cooperation for Space Standardisation
EEIG	European Economic Interest Groupings
EGNOS	European Geostationnary Navigation Overlay System
EIB	European Investment Bank
ELDO	European space vehicle Launcher Development Organisation
ERNP	European Radionavigation Plan
ERS	European Remote Sensing Satellite
ESA	European Space Agency
ESRO	European Space Research Organisation
ETG	European Tripartite Group
ETSI	European Telecommunications Standards Institute
EUMETSAT	EUropean organisation for the exploitation of METeo. SATellites
EUROCONTROL	European Association for Air Traffic Control
EUROGOOS	EUROpean Global Ocean Observing System

EUROSPACE	EUROpean SPACE industry association
FOC	Full Operational Capability
GLONASS	GLObal NAvigation System Satellite
GNSS	Global Navigation Satellite System
GOOS	Global Ocean Observing System
GPS	Global Positioning System
ICAO	International Civil Aviation Organisation
IMO	International Maritime Organisation
INMARSAT	INternational MARitime SATellite organisation
ITU	International Telecommunication Union
METEOSAT	METEOrological SATellite
NIS	New Independent States
PCS	Personal Communications Services
SAG	Space Advisory Group
SME	Small and Medium-sized Entreprise
SPOT	Satellite Pour l'Observation de la Terre
TACIS	Technical Assistance for the CIS
UMTS	Universal Mobile Telephony Service
VSAT	Very Small Aperture Terminals
WEU	West European Union
WTO	World Trade Organisation

Acknowledgements:

Many of the photos used in this publication were supplied
courtesy of the European Space Agency (ESA).

European Commission

The European Union and Space – Fostering applications, markets and industrial competitiveness

Luxembourg: Office for Official Publications of the European Communities

1997 – 56 pp. – 17,6 x 25 cm

ISBN 92-827-9262-5

Price (excluding VAT) in Luxembourg: ECU 7